Build Your Own Still

Learn to Make Water, Fuel, Alcohol and More

by Tristan Trubble

Published in USA by:

Tristan Trubble
P.O BOX #9
Boynton Beach
FL 33425

© Copyright 2016

ISBN-13: 978-1540346018
ISBN-10: 1540346013

Table of Contents

Why You Would Want to Build a Still

Hello folks! Tristan Trubble here bringing you another informative and educational eBook on how to properly construct your own moonshine making still.

There are a couple of different reasons you might want to build a still. Making moonshine can be a very exciting and rewarding experience. It can also be a very hazardous industry to become involved with, especially from a legal stand point. Most of the old timers make moonshine for personal consumption as well as profit. Some do it because it has been a family business for several generations.

In the modern era people enjoy being able to make moonshine because it is cheaper than purchasing store bought, name brand beverages. Some of them do it for fun, or to provide for them and their family and friends, while others continue to try and make a living from brewing illicit beverages that cannot be found on store shelves.

Each person will have their personal reasons for diving into the home distillation opportunity. It might be something you just want to see if you can do out of inquisitive curiosity, or it could be an idea you have as a part time hobby. It might be something you have wanted to do for as long as you can remember, or it might be a brand new concept.

One idea would involve stocking a supply of 'Holiday Hooch.' If you have a secret sour mash recipe that you like to share with the family during seasonal gatherings, then building your own still more than likely appeals to you.

Another aspect of consideration might be to produce moonshine as a currency equivalent. Several people that are prepping for a possible doomsday theorize that grain alcohol will be a valuable commodity in a post-apocalyptic new world society. In this scenario moonshine will be used as a bargaining tool to trade for goods and services. Those that know how to make it will be in high demand, as well as have an upper hand in the new economy.

If you are considering being prepared for the future you should give some serious consideration to building your own still. You don't even have to enjoy alcohol or drink it for that matter; you just need to know how to be on the supply end of the demand chain.

Life in a survival of the fittest atmosphere will be a lot easier to handle if you have the ability to barter for the things you need effectively. Nobody is going to be hospitable and happy to hand out their own supplies to provide for those that are helpless. It will be a brutal and grim environment under the best of circumstances, not a place for the meek or ill-prepared.

Your reasons for wanting to make homemade hooch should remain as clandestine as the location of your cauldron regardless of what they are. The fewer people that know about the operation of your still the safer and more secure it will be.

Starting From Scratch

Before you run out to the tool shed to see what tools and supplies you have available for manufacturing a device of this nature, take a few minutes to determine what you will need. Designing and building a still involves a number of different decisions that need to be addressed before the process can begin.

You will want to take the time to consider where your still is going to be located and what type of still you prefer to own and operate. You may also want to invest in our other eBook, titled "How to Make Moonshine," before you make a selection on what type of still you would like to construct.

Still designs and diagrams encompass a wide variety of possible solutions. There are stove top stills, pot stills, reflux stills, as well as different ideas on stills for making moonshine, beer, or wine. The potent potable you have a preference for making will narrow the field of selection somewhat, but it will not eliminate all of the possibilities.

Manufacturing moonshine, whiskey, beer, and/or wine can be done legally or illegally, depending on the brewer's desires. In order to perform your operation legally you will have to apply for a permit and license. Once you are approved you will be issued the proper paperwork to keep you from being punished or penalized for distilling spirits. Keep in mind that this approach involves paying taxes, and often takes several months or years to fight through all of the red tape to get the paperwork required. Illegal operators can avoid the wait but the penalties and fines for getting caught are extremely stiff.

Selecting a location for housing your still is going to be an important part of the planning process as well. If you are applying for the permits to operate, then location will not be as much of a concern. If, on the other hand, you will be operating on the wrong side of the legal fence so to speak, then the placement of your still will be of utmost importance. You're going to want to find a spot that is off the beaten path and difficult to discover.

It will also be important to plan your purchases of the equipment, tools, and supplies that you will need. Any of the tools that you will need can be purchased from the same hardware store; however you may want to purchase the still supplies from a variety of resources in order to keep your shopping habits from appearing on Big Brother's radar. Make no mistake about it; government agencies such as the BATF will use every device at their disposal to find out where illegal liquor is being made.

Modern technology in the commercial market place of general merchandise has evolved. In many cases if you buy your supplies, tools, equipment, and ingredients from any big, name brand box stores the computerized cash registers will track and record your shopping habits, especially if you pay for the products with a credit or debit card. If you buy in bulk, then pay with cash, and neglect any offers to register or sign up for additional services with the store.

Oak Barrels for Storage

Deciding on the Right Size & Style

Before you do anything else you need to determine where your still will be located. This area will ultimately decide how big or small your still can be. If the purpose behind making moonshine is for personal use you might elect to perform all procedures within the house. In this case a small stove top still or pot still might be in order. You can build one of these in a relatively short period of time and depending on the style you elect to go with, you might be able to dismantle the device when it is not in use, rather than have to risk leaving it together and getting caught.

The size and style of the still will also determine how much moonshine can be made at any given time. Smaller models will be sufficient for the home brewer producing for personal use; however they may not produce the quantity desired for those that intend to share or supply others with their high quality octane.

If you have never built a still for making moonshine before, you may want to start off building a small system to begin with. You can always build a bigger model at a later date if desired. By beginning with a small compact system you can perfect the process, and if you have a little ingenuity you may find it easier to modify bigger design plans to suit your needs.

Keep in mind that covertness is commonplace for moonshine makers regardless of whether they are doing things legally or illegally. Even if you have taken the necessary steps to secure the proper paperwork you may find yourself visited periodically by government employees to ensure you are keeping within the letter of the law. As a matter of fact owning and operating a moonshine making machine legally might result in a higher profile than doing so illegally.

The budget you have set aside for a project of this nature might also prevent you from constructing a sizeable still at the onset. For brand new nectar concocting prodigies, it is highly recommended to minimize expenses until such a time as you are comfortable and confident with how to properly operate a still system. Unless you have an engineering degree, coupled with a science specialty, you are not going to build your first still and become an overnight moonshine making master. It will take years of trial and error experience before you develop the talent to produce a perfect, potent, and palatable potion.

For the purpose of simplifying construction instructions we are going to be providing the necessary information for building a small yet effective distillery. This device can be used in either an indoor or outdoor location, provided caution and care are taken into account. This design will be a useful stepping stone for the Do It Yourself denizen that can get them started in the manufacturing for personal use process.

Making a List of Materials, Supplies & Tools

I know some of you are thinking that making a list is a time consuming process that should be easily eliminated in this day and age. That couldn't be further from the truth. Making a list is an essential part of the process. It will prevent you from having to make several return trips to the hardware or supply store to pick up the items you forgot the first time. Remember, you are trying to keep a low profile, returning to the same store several times a day to make an additional purchase can send off alarms and warning bells to those that would otherwise remain unaware of what your intentions are.

The first item on the list is going to serve as the kettle for the shine making system. You can use a large stainless steel or copper pot with a lid. The size of the pot will determine the amount of sour mash alcohol that can be produced in a single run. Make sure this pot will be big enough to incorporate the necessary ingredients for the recipe you are following.

You will also need copper tubing. This tubing needs to be pure copper, not an alloyed or copper coated substitute. This copper tubing will come in direct contact with the vapor that will burn off the mash and ultimately result in the honeyed nectar known as moonshine. If the tubing is not pure copper the vapor that forms within will, at some point in time, begin to expose harmful materials to the liquor and pollute the potions it produces. This tubing should be at least a ½" in diameter and at least 6' long.

A cooking thermometer will also come in handy. This gauge needs to be able to encompass temperatures in excess of $212°$ F. It should also have a puncturing point for insertion. It doesn't have to be anything fancy; it just has to function properly.

Buy a large round rubber stopper with a 2" - 3" diameter. Make sure it is big enough that you can drill two separate holes in it. This device will house both the thermometer and one end of the copper tubing.

A power drill and a reciprocating saw with metal cutting bits and blades will also be necessary. These tools will cut the hole in the kettle lid to fit the rubber stopper.

Add a soldering iron, silver solder solution, or caulk gun and water tight sealant to the list. These will be used to permanently seal various parts of the alcohol concocting containers.

Clamping equipment or vises will be helpful for coiling the copper tubing. A solid object with about a 3" diameter will make coiling the copper tubing easier to accommodate.

A small pocket knife should always be kept close at hand to assist in making miniature modifications such as shaving off a little extra rubber on the stopper or to help with wedging the stopper into the lid.

A carboy, whiskey jug, or glass jars with sealing lids will round out the list. These will be used for collecting and storage of the hooch once it has been distilled from the mash.

Old Fashioned Moonshine Setup

Advantages & Disadvantages of Power Tools vs. Hand Tools

As part of the overall planning process you may want to consider what types of tools you will be using to perform the construction of your still. There are advantages and disadvantages associated with using either hand tools or power tools.

The advantages of using power tools are rather obvious. It makes the process of drilling and cutting holes a heck of a lot easier. In so doing they also reduce the amount of time involved with the entire construction process. The disadvantages of using power tools are somewhat less easy to immediately identify. The biggest disadvantage associated with power tools being you need a suitable power source to supply them. Battery operated drills and saws are mobile but they require recharging periodically. If you are going to be building your still on site, in the nether regions of the back forty, this could pose a problem.

Another disadvantage with using power tools is that they need to be stored in a warm, dry place when not in use. They are extremely temperamental to inclement weather conditions or harsh environments such as sand and mud, tree sap, and other conditions that exist in the great outdoors. If they are left exposed to the weather they can quit working altogether and resemble and overpriced paperweight. Manually operated tools may become rusty if exposed to the elements, but in most cases they can still be used when and if needed.

The advantages of using hand tools are that they are easier to transport. They are cheaper and easier to replace should they become broken or ineffective. If they are accidentally left on site they are less likely to be stolen, or fail due to weather exposure.

If you have an eye on the future and possible apocalyptic events, then hand tools will also have the advantage of being useful in such a situation. Should the day ever arrive that electricity is unavailable, power tools will last as long as the current battery life, after which they will become nothing more than cumbersome objects to carry.

You are probably asking yourself who in their right mind would attempt to hand drill a 3" hole into the lid of a copper kettle, and you would be right, not too many people would. In a post-apocalyptic environment you will not need to hand drill holes in metal lids but you will need to hand drill holes in the rubber stopper. The holes for the lid can be cut using an acetylene torch, and you can believe there will be plenty of these around. Cutting torches do not require electricity to operate; all you will need to do is find one, which shouldn't be very difficult. Look in the local phone book for an address to the nearest distributor, there will be plenty of supplies waiting to be used.

Use power tools while you can but be prepared and knowledgeable about what to use should power become unavailable. Surviving the apocalypse will require you to abide by the age old adage; 'Where there is a will, there is a way.

Configuring Your Still According to Site Location

You need to build your still according to the available size of your site location. If you are cooking the concoction on your stove top the supplies listed above will suffice. If you are selecting an outdoor area for setting up the still you may need more than 6' of copper tubing to reach from the kettle to the carboy.

Interior kettle cooking and moonshine manufacturing will limit the size of the pot and the amount of available space. This may be important depending on how big of a batch you want to brew. The general rule is that for every 5 gallons of mash you can expect to produce approximately 3 quarts of quality product in the neighborhood of 40% alcohol. The more space you have available the bigger cauldron you can cook with.

If you are going to be boiling outside, then you need to keep in mind the flammable properties associated with making moonshine. You will want to place the collection container in a location far enough away from the kettle to prevent possible ignition. Always remember that the sour mash solution is going to be exposed to extreme temperatures in the $175°$ F - $215°$ F range. It will also produce highly ignitable vapors that will travel the length of the copper tube to the collection chamber. Any leaks along the system can pose a potential problem immediately.

Outdoor locations can encompass a wide variety of elevations along the terrain. This will also be important since you should construct an outdoor still on site, especially if you are trying to keep it in a covert corner of the country. All of the materials and tools will need to be transported to this location. The moonshining industry has always been associated with hill side still sites. If you are choosing this type of environment you will want to ensure that you build the still so that the carboy collecting the finished product is kept at a lower elevation.

Dig the fire pit in at a higher altitude and use as much copper coiled tubing as necessary to reach the storage jar or jug. If/when fire spreads it travels uphill before blazing in a downward direction under most circumstances. Pay attention to general wind direction and local weather patterns. High wind areas will push a fire downhill just as rapidly, if not more so, than it would under normal conditions.

Decide if your still is going to be a permanent fixture or a temporary solution. If you are going to be boiling your beverage in the back yard, you might want to use a still that is small enough to store in the back corner of the tool shed when not in use. The same applies for those building a stove top still for interior use. Not only should the cooking area be able to handle the contraption, there should be ample storage space in a closet or attic for keeping the instrument intact when it isn't being put to good use.

Step by Step Still Setup

Step #1: Grab the lid, the drill, and the reciprocating saw. Ensure that metal cutting blades and bits are in place. Drill a hole in the middle of the lid big enough to fit the rubber stopper in place. Try to keep this hole slightly smaller than the stopper so that it can be squeezed into place and fit snugly and securely. If you hack a hole in place don't throw it away and start over; that's what the caulk is for, just make sure the hatchet job isn't so bad that the caulk is going to be exposed to the interior of the kettle and you will be fine.

Step #2: Grab the rubber stopper. You already have the drill handy so drill a hole to fit the copper tubing and the thermometer. These holes should also provide a snug fit for the device being inserted.

Step #3: Take the copper tubing, clamping or vise devices, and the solid 3" diameter object you have chosen. Leave at least 18" of straight length at each end. Use the clamps and grips to coil the copper tube around the solid object until nothing but the two straight ends are all that remains. There is no standard to be concerned with as far as how many coils are required. If your still configuration is going to require more than the recommended 6' length, then buy a longer length to begin with, don't waste time trying to solder joints into the system, it will only complicate matters.

Step #4: Attach and seal the lid. If you are handy with a soldering iron, then use it to craft a permanent seal around the lid. If soldering capabilities escape you, then forego them and grab the caulking gun and waterproof sealant. Clamp the lid in place and apply the caulk. It doesn't have to be professional quality just so long as it fills the gaps. You can check this seal once the caulk dries by filling the kettle with water and test firing it. Plug the hole in the lid with the rubber stopper. If no steam escapes, then the seal is perfect.

Step #5: Remove contents of the kettle, replace the rubber stopper, fit one end of the copper tube into the appropriate hole, fit the thermometer into the other orifice and caulk any gaps that may be present. Run a little around each fitting just to be safe.

Step #6: Take the carboy, whiskey jug, or whatever collection container you have available and place it wherever you will be setting it. Insert the other end of the copper tube into the top of this collection and storage container.

At this point you are basically ready to begin making moonshine. All you need to do now is decide on a recipe, obtain the ingredients and follow the instructions that come with it. If all of your fittings are solid you should produce a satisfying batch of homemade hooch.

Earthen Jug for Collection & Storage

Indoor vs. Outdoor Solutions

There are advantages to making moonshine in either an indoor or outdoor setting. There are also disadvantages associated with either option.

An indoor solution will allow you to maintain a low profile for the purpose. You won't have to camouflage or disguise your activities as much as you would running through the woods. A small stove top still can be a very effective moonshine manufacturing system. It can also be stored in a location out of sight from visitors when desired.

Operating an indoor still does limit your ability to produce larger quantities but that is a small price to pay as far as the bigger picture is concerned. Making moonshine is still illegal without procuring the proper permits so low visibility is always something to consider seriously.

Inside operated stills also provide a level of comfort in regards to safety and security. You won't have to make constant and continuous trips to an outside location, or spend countless hours away from home to monitor the distillation process. All of your materials, tools, supplies, ingredients and stock can be kept in one convenient location under your control at all times.

An outside still does provide some advantages as well. Depending on the location of the site it may be very difficult for someone who happens to stumble upon it to identify who it belongs to. If you feel as though the site has been discovered, then you can abandon it and let the heat subside before beginning in a new location.

Operating an outside still will also prevent the possibility of allowing a hazardous situation from destroying your entire house. Potential fire hazards are always possible regardless of where the boiling and distillation takes place; however if such an event occurs in an outdoor location it may be contained before it can cause significant irreparable damage.

The owner and operator of an outdoor moonshine manufacturing facility will also protect the members of their family from possibly being charged with a criminal offense should they be caught. An illegal still operated inside the residence subjects the entire property to forfeiture and all occupants to accomplice charges.

Outdoor fires will need to be constantly and continuously monitored and fed in order to maintain temperature during distillation. This can be very time consuming and tedious when compared to an indoor solution which can be monitored and maintained with slight adjustments to flame height on the stove or burner.

These are all topics you will want to consider and apply carefully to your current conditions. If you are borderline agoraphobic and seldom set foot outside of your house, then suddenly spending every afternoon at the back end of your heavily wooded lot is going to attract the attention of your nosy neighborhood watchdog types. Choose your site wisely and in conjunction with your current established habits.

Designing the Diagram

Why would it be necessary to design a diagram for a homemade still in this day and age of information and technology? There are a couple of good reasons actually that are well worth the investment of time to draw out a diagram of the still design you are confident in building.

The primary reason is so that it can be used as an instructional and educational schematic. This will come in handy regardless of where you set up your still, but especially for the outdoor enthusiast. The last thing you want to do is forget a crucial or vital step in the construction process. Rather than carry around several pages of literature and instructions, a single sheet of paper with a detailed design can be stored in a pocket until it is needed.

Another possible reason would be to prevent taking things for granted. People tend to rely too much on technology and modern capabilities such as electricity. While it is currently possible to discover any and all information about a given topic by accessing the internet, this does not necessarily mean that we will always have these advantages at our disposal. In the event of a catastrophic collapse of the power grid, computers and the internet will be non-existent overnight. If you don't have a detailed diagram handy to help you in the aftermath, then you may not be able to locate relevant information at the local library.

Diagrams are basically pictures and pictures say a thousand words, or so they say. They are easier to interpret and follow if drawn well, than in depth detailed descriptions included in several pages of instructions.

You do not have to be Michelangelo to design a diagram of the still you decide to build. As long as it is legible to you it will suffice to serve as a blueprint for success. Even if you feel completely confident in your abilities to remember every detail of the instructions you have read to construct a copper kettle still, a diagram will ensure that the finished product appears as it should.

You might want to consider making a couple copies of the still drawing and design just as a precautionary measure. Even if the world doesn't end tomorrow web sites come and go, the information you found for building the still several months ago may have been recently removed or replaced. If you have your own schematic handy you won't have to worry about coming up with a whole new design.

Keep it simple yet effective. Do not overpopulate the page with a heavy hand and write down so much information it becomes cluttered and confusing to decipher.

Hazards of Improper Construction Procedures

Regardless of what type of still you decide to build you need to ensure you attempt to adhere to the directions provided by the original designer. Implementing shortcuts, substituting materials, or attempting to circumvent a particular step in the process, can result in property damage, personal injury, or even death. These hazards are multiplied and magnified for those that are building a still by hand as opposed to purchasing a kit or prefabricated system.

Use only the materials described by the inventor of the design unless you have a very valid reason to believe it may be incorrect. Do not, under any circumstances use metal alloys for any part of the construction process. Alloys can create harmful situations to the finished supply making it unsuitable for human consumption. Depending on the circumstances the potent potable may also end up being fatal. Pure copper, stainless steel, and silver for soldering are the only acceptable materials for creating a fully functional and safe still.

Making moonshine requires boiling which in turn requires a heat source. The majority of you will be using a flame of some sort either on top of the stove or in a fire pit. Poorly constructed stills that have leaks along the line can erupt in flame or explode altogether. In an explosive situation shrapnel will be present. You can imagine the amount of damage that can occur under these circumstances. Take the time to make sure your cauldron is well-crafted and constructed.

Leaky cauldrons will also cause inconsistency in quality of the alcoholic concoction. While this may not seem like much of a hazard for the personal consumption specialist, those that are using moonshine to make additional money will notice a steadily declining level of clients. Producing for profit requires near perfect consistency.

Building a moonshine machine is not the place to pull out your Cracker Jack Engineering degree to make modifications you think will enhance the features of the equipment. If you want to mess around with the style, design, and function of the still, then make sure you test fire the system with straight water before using a mash mixture. Straight water will boil and produce steam that will vaporize along the copper tube and deposit in the collection chamber.

If your still design is sloppy, or your seals aren't secure, then you are going to harm yourself and others before you ever make a drinkable batch of moonshine. You are reading a "How to" book about the right way to do things because this isn't a birdhouse; you can't just slap it together, throw some grain in it and walk away. If it were that easy there wouldn't be any money in it for the major distilleries.

If you want to make moonshine, then take every precautionary step you can think of, leave nothing to chance. An ounce of prevention is worth a pound of cure!

Keeping Your Still Location Secret

Why is it necessary to keep your still location secret? Well, for starters, if you do not possess the proper legal documentation to own or operate a moonshine making still, then you are functioning illegally. The penalties for conducting such operations can be very stiff, up to and including forfeiture of property, as well as extended prison sentences.

In order to avoid becoming a blip on the radar screen of the local, state, or federal policing agencies it will behoove you to keep the lowest profile possible. Advertising your abilities and moonshine making capabilities is akin to inviting disaster.

Due to the illicit and illegal nature of the moonshining industry there are plenty of people that would like to stumble upon a still or know where one is located. If you want to protect and maintain your still you will want to avoid attracting unwanted attention. The more people that know about your little operation the greater chance you have of showing up one day to an empty storage space. You will have to bite the bullet and accept the sacrifice as a learning experience because filing a complaint at the local cop shop is not going to be an available option unless you have an officer that is a loyal customer.

Keeping the still location a well-guarded secret will provide as much safety and security as can be expected. This doesn't mean it will never be found, especially if it is located in an outdoor location that can be accessed by anyone with an interest in walking through the woods. You may want to establish preventive precautions to ensure your safety when working with a woodland still. Set up a few non-lethal booby traps around the area to ward off would be onlookers; you'd be surprised how many people will shy away from an area that has been doused with doe urine simply because of the smell.

Do not set up an established routine of visiting the still site. A scheduled routine is one of the easiest ways to get caught. Anyone that has a small suspicion about what you are doing will be able to figure out your course of action and discover what you are doing. Vary the times you go to the still as well as the times you return. Establish a few different routes for getting into and out of the area. Never use the same access point on a regular basis. Three or four avenues should suffice.

If you have a dog, then take them with you from time to time. Pets of this nature are highly sensitive to their surroundings and can alert you to any possible intrusions. They will alert to smells they are unfamiliar with as well as noises that are too far away for a human to hear. They will let you know if the coast is clear or if there is potential trouble waiting.

A good rule of thumb to follow is that for every person you share the secret with, they will share it with at least one other, and the domino effect will continue. There are two rules to keeping a secret; #1) Never tell anyone everything you know. If you are looking for rule number two, then you misunderstood rule number one.

Shiner walking out to the Still Site

Camouflaging Equipment

Depending on where you decide to place your still you may want to take the time to install some camouflage to help keep it hidden. You don't have to actually go out and purchase netting or other material to create a safe haven for your still. Use the natural surroundings to help blend the site into the background.

If you are going to be distilling from the comfort of the back yard, or a relatively close location, then you might want to consider using a small storage shed or something similar just to keep it from being seen by the naked eye of a curious passerby.

Once you learn the basics of constructing a still you can get creative with camouflaging techniques. You would be surprised at how many people have fully functioning moonshine stills sitting in plain sight. They disguise them to look like everyday objects that go unnoticed by the average person.

Use your imagination during the design and try to make it look as natural as possible. You don't want to construct camouflage that makes someone want to investigate further. In other words, don't make it look man made, broken branches do not fall from trees and align themselves perfectly around an area or object.

Consider taking a chainsaw with you and cutting down some lumber, you will need a fuel source for the fire anyway and if done correctly you can make the area appear as though it is being thinned out. Use the fallen branches as a blockade to redirect any unforeseen traffic in a different direction.

If you have the time and tools as well as the drive, determination, and desire you can always excavate a nice like niche into the hillside and create a cavern for your cauldron. You will have to install a venting tube through the top to allow the release of smoke from the fire but the entrance to a cave is going to be harder to find than an open area still site.

Another option worth considering might be building a ghillie style suit to wrap around a few surrounding trees to create a more natural looking canvas. You will need to purchase the netting and craft your own design from natural foliage found in the immediate area; however when applied proficiently this method will make the site almost invisible to the untrained eye.

Stocking & Storing Replacement Parts

In this section we are going to cover the reasons you might want to stock spare parts and store them in a safe place.

If you have an abundance of spare parts for your still stored in a safe place you can minimize the amount of down time should something decide to break or become inoperable. Moonshine stills are subjected to intense pressure during the distillation process. Some manufacturers of the equipment used in still construction use lower standards during the production process, these parts can fail slowly over time or without forewarning. If you have the right parts already in store, then fixing the problem will be significantly easier and allow you to continue making moonshine without too much of a delay.

Spare parts can also be used to construct additional stills to be situated in various places or for concocting different qualities and kinds of grain alcohol at the same time. If you only have one still you are only going to be brewing one batch at a time.

If you are going to be taking moonshining seriously, then you will want to have several stills available at your disposal. You can begin the adventure by building your first still and while learning how to operate it effectively you can busy yourself with building another still to use for a different potion or to increase your current supply capabilities.

For those that have a prepping mentality, stocking and storing supplies of this nature may be a necessary inclusion in the planning process. These items can be used in the aftermath as trade bait for bartering. You might want to offer to build a still for another survivor in exchange for other goods or services. They might also be useful in allowing you to establish stills across a wider region and use the supplies in the same bartering fashion to secure payments for traded goods.

Of course in an aftermarket apocalyptic atmosphere it won't be necessary to store and stock these supplies as they should be readily available at several general merchandise stores. Not many survivors will be interested in material objects that have no value and copper tubing, stainless steel pots, and carboys or whiskey jugs, aren't going to be in very high demand, at least not until you show people what they can do with them. It still wouldn't be a bad idea to get a jump on the competition and secure the items you will need while they are still being produced.

In a survivalist scenario you will want to continue prepping for the future, look for the items you need in out of the way places. Visit the manufacturing plants where products like copper tubing and kettles are made, there should be plenty lying around. Stop by restaurants, electrical supply companies, and hardware stores to search for resources to restock your supplies.

Fine Tuning the Manufacturing Process

Once you have properly built your first fully functional moonshine making machine it is time to start fine tuning the manufacturing process. If you develop a passion for producing potent and palatable potions of an alcoholic nature, then your first still won't be your last still. Being able to put a still together in a relatively short period of time may be beneficial to you in the future, especially if the first one becomes damaged or is being used for a specific mixture.

To fine tune and master the construction process you will need to consider buying the list of necessary supplies in bulk. These spare parts can be used to create templates for future still making endeavors. You might have to go through the process several times before developing a plan you want to use as a template. When you have a solid design to go by the process of putting together a still will be significantly easier and less time consuming.

Over time you will develop the talent to implement your own tweaks to the design and modify the moonshine still to your preferences. If you decide to use a different type or style of still for future distillation then you will want to repeat this process.

A still should be effective and efficient. The first still you build may turn out looking rather crude and rudimentary compared to one you build after mastering the technique. There are hundreds of still designs to choose from and while the information offered here was for a small version suitable for stove top or fire pit use, they all involve the same basic concepts. You will need a sealed kettle to boil mash in, copper tubing for collecting the condensation and a catch can for storing the final solution.

There are several options available for modifying a still. Depending on how polished an appearance you would like the finished product to have you might decide to use copper flaring equipment and locking nuts to establish a removable effective seal for the coiled copper. You will have modified the lid of the kettle to accommodate threading the locking nut but that is not an entirely unimaginable concept either.

Those of you that are new to the process of still construction are advised to save the drastic overhaul of the design plan for a few years. Get familiar with operating a still before going out on a limb and dreaming up your own design. Many moonshiners have tried and failed to build a still simply because they think they have a better idea or opinion on how something should be done. Short of being a moonshine making savant you will need to study the inner workings of the still system you are using before you can begin to come up with ideas on what might make it work more effectively.

Any immediate modifications to an established and

proven still design should be minimal in nature and always tested before put into normal mash making operation. Major modifications could lead to disaster no matter how well thought out they may seem. Make a few minor tweaks here and there, water test the system, make a few more adjustments and continue repeating the process until you have reached the final design you were trying to obtain.

DISCLAIMER AND/OR LEGAL NOTICES: Every effort has been made to accurately represent this book and it's potential. Results vary with every individual, and your results may or may not be different from those depicted. No promises, guarantees or warranties, whether stated or implied, have been made that you will produce any specific result from this book. Your efforts are individual and unique, and may vary from those shown. Your success depends on your efforts, background and motivation.

The material in this publication is provided for educational and informational purposes only and is not intended as medical advice. The information contained in this book should not be used to diagnose or treat any illness, metabolic disorder, disease or health problem. Always consult your physician or health care provider before beginning any nutrition or exercise program. Use of the programs, advice, and information contained in this book is at the sole choice and risk of the reader.

Manufactured by Amazon.ca
Acheson, AB

15680263R00026